# THE HAPPIEST BOY ON EARTH

# THE HAPPIEST BOY ON EARTH

## Eddie Jaku
### illustrated by Nathaniel Eckstrom

MACMILLAN
**Pan Macmillan Australia**

Pan Macmillan acknowledges the Traditional Custodians of country
throughout Australia and their connections to lands, waters and
communities. We pay our respect to Elders past and present and extend
that respect to all Aboriginal and Torres Strait Islander peoples today.
We honour more than sixty thousand years of storytelling, art and culture.

First published 2022 in Macmillan by Pan Macmillan Australia Pty Ltd
Based on *The Happiest Man on Earth* published 2020 by Pan Macmillan Australia Pty Ltd
1 Market Street, Sydney, New South Wales, Australia, 2000

Text copyright © Eddie Jaku 2022
Illustration copyright © Nathaniel Eckstrom © 2022
Text adaptation by Donna Rawlins

 A catalogue record for this
book is available from the
National Library of Australia

Design by Melanie Feddersen, i2i design
Colour reproduction by Splitting Image Colour Studio
Printed in China by Imago

10 9 8 7 6 5 4 3 2 1

For future generations

*Pépé! We're here! We're here!*

This is my favourite sound. The rowdy noise of my great-grandchildren stampeding to meet me at my door. Me. Eddie. 'Pépé' to them. One hundred and one years old – and the happiest man on Earth.

It's always a good day when the house is full of family
and friends – and cake. And what a cake – pineapple!

*Tell us about your pineapple again, Pépé.*

Well, I was in Leipzig where I grew up with my mother, father, my little sister Henni, and our grandmother – such a happy family in such a beautiful city. There was theatre, and music and art, galleries full of masterpieces, and opera – the grown-ups loved the opera! And the university – it was built in 1409 – imagine that! Even I wasn't around then!

*You're funny, Pépé!*

But most of all, I loved the zoo. We lived just five minutes' walk from more lions than anywhere outside the plains of Africa.

*Did you hear them roaring at night?*
*But what about Lulu? Tell us about Lulu.*

Of course. Lulu. She was the most adorable
dachshund who ever yapped and licked.

I had everything I could ever want.

But, there came a time when it was hard to get even simple things – bread, fruit . . . You don't notice things like that when you are a child. Your lives are full of changes. Your shoes become tight, your sleeves become short.

But my parents knew other things were changing – everywhere in our city. Grown-ups have a way of knowing that.

On Fridays, my mother baked delicious challah loaves, more
than we needed, and shared what we had with other families.

Then, when my birthday was close, my lovely father asked what gift I would like. Well, my stomach chose for me. I asked for six eggs, a loaf of white bread – something very special in Germany – and a rare tropical fruit – a pineapple! And somehow, my father managed to find these precious things for me. I was the happiest boy on Earth.

You will not be surprised to hear that I ate them all at once. And a whole pineapple. Then I had one more thing for my birthday – a tummy ache!

*What about your next birthday, Pépé?*
*What did you ask for then?*

Ah. Well, everything was very different by then. It wasn't just white bread and pineapples that were hard to find. Even the simplest things began to disappear.

Into the sunshine of my childhood crept a dark,
heavy cloud – not a rain cloud – worse than that.

People all over Germany were angry – they had
no jobs and no money.

When people are unhappy, you know,
they will often look for someone else to blame.

This happened in Leipzig. It happened in Hamburg. In Munich –
in Hanover and Berlin. All over Germany many people started to listen to
a dangerous and angry man called Hitler. Even in the tiniest villages the
desperate townsfolk, like those in all the cities, began to blame the Jewish
people – not because we had done anything wrong – but because we
were different from them.

This still happens today all over the world, but never be suspicious of
people just because they seem different from you, my young ones.
This is how wars begin.

*What happened, Pépé?*

Jewish children were thrown out of their schools. Imagine!
I loved school. In the winter, when the river froze over,
I could skate there in five minutes!

When I was little I wanted to be a doctor when I grew up, but I was also curious to learn how things work. In those days, students were tested to see what they were especially good at and, when I was 13, we discovered that I would make a fine engineer. So when I was banned from going to school, I thought my dreams were over.

But my clever father had a plan. He found a boarding school nine hours'
train ride from our home. He gave me a 'new' German name,
Walter Schleif, and he sent me away to learn – a secret Jewish boy
with the name of a gentile – pretending to be an orphan.

*Were you afraid, Pépé?*

Of course. I was terrified! I was scared and homesick and lonely, but I had no choice.

So, you see, if I had wanted anything at all for my
next birthday, it would simply have been to see my family.
I missed them every day of my life.

But I studied hard – for my father and mother, and for myself.

I was awarded an apprenticeship, and so I worked and learned in the day and attended extra classes at night. Mathematics and science, engineering and mechanics fascinated me. Perhaps I would be an inventor?

When you are a child, your elders tell you how important education is. It's hard to understand this now. But believe me, when YOU are 101 years old, you too will look back on the amazing journey of your life and recognise the map you began to draw for it. Your education will lead you to astonishing places – and may even save your life.

By the time I was 18, I was crafting very advanced and clever medical equipment. So you see, I was an inventor after all, and I made tools for the doctors I had always admired. In a way, I was helping them to save lives.

*Were your parents proud of you, Pépé?*

Oh, yes. But in those days, the only way
you could communicate with people far
away was by letters and, sometimes,
a telephone call from a public phone.
But I had to be careful that no-one would
ever catch me with a letter addressed to
a Jewish family, so I hardly ever contacted them.

One day, after five years away, I decided to surprise my family and visit them. I travelled for many hours by train, right across Germany. But when I finally reached our family home in Leipzig, it was empty.

My family had gone.

*But where, Pépé?*

I had no idea.

There were many things I didn't know. I had been so busy with my work, I hadn't seen life growing darker and more frightening in Germany. I hadn't learned exactly how dangerous it had become to be a Jew.

Thinking I was safely away from all the trouble in Leipzig, my family had fled to safety. For a while, at least.

That night, I lay down to sleep in my childhood bed.

But as I slept, on the other side of the city, mobs of angry people were rioting, rampaging, and smashing the windows of shops, synagogues and houses belonging to Jewish people. They were burning and destroying everything, leaving a glistening, razor-sharp carpet of broken glass all over the streets.

Today we call that night *Kristallnacht*: the Night of Broken Glass.

At five o'clock that morning, I was woken by the terrifying sound of our front door being knocked down by Nazi soldiers.
They captured me, beat me, and took me away.

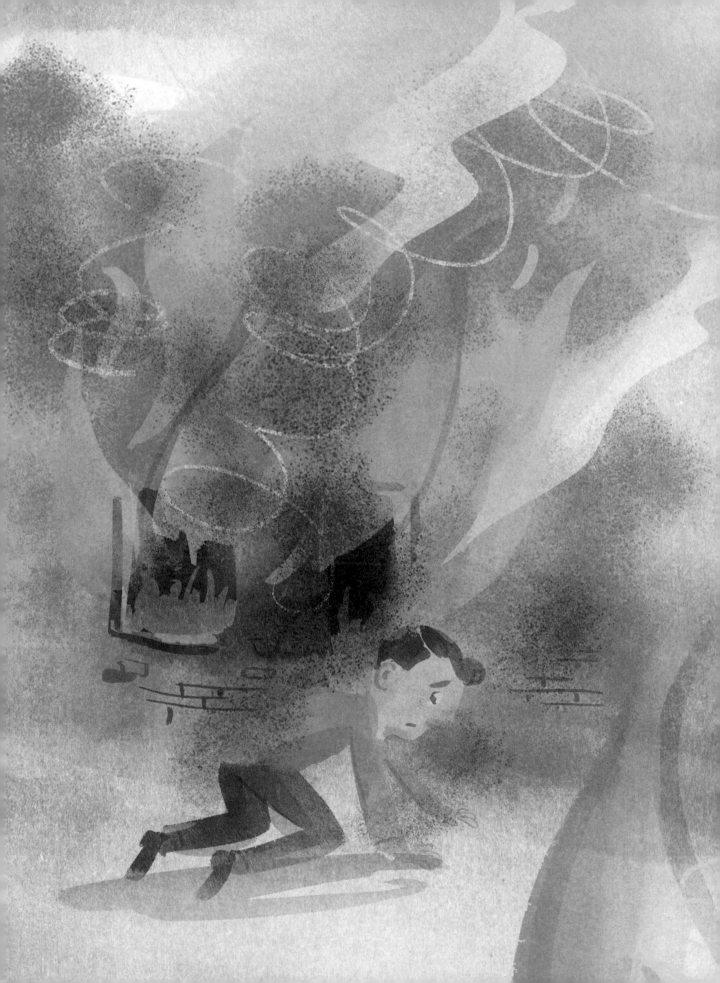

*Pépé! How scared you must have been.*

I was. Very scared. That was the day I lost many things but, most importantly, I lost my faith in humankind and my freedom.

*But, Pépé, you are here now.*

Yes I am, indeed! And if I had not been rescued by the kindness of strangers I would not be here – and neither would you, my curious great-grandchildren!

I was taken to a terrible place – a camp overflowing with misery and surrounded by barbed wire. The guards were very cruel. They treated Jews as though we were criminals. Families were separated, old from young, women and girls from men and boys. Many of us never saw our families again. Many of us were killed, or grew sick from hunger and disease. And some wanted to die because they lost all hope.

Sometimes we were moved to other camps, trudging through the snow, and prodded all the while by the Nazi soldiers shouting and pushing us forward. Many died on those marches.

It was long ago, and far away, but the memories never fade.

*I would cry, Pépé. But you were so brave!*

Oh, I cried, believe me. I cried for my mother and father, for my sister Henni, for my grandmother, for little Lulu. I cried for all the people around me suffering and dying. I cried for what I had lost and what might have been.

We are all the same, you see. Everyone in the world – children and adults, gentiles and Jews. We all feel fear and loss, pain and sadness. Mostly, I cried that there were people who had forgotten that we are all the same – all equal – all deserving of dignity, kindness and freedom.

*Did you give up hope, Pépé?*

For some time, I thought I would lose hope, but I held on tight to it because hope for the heart is like food for the belly. It nourishes us and sustains us. It helps us take the next breath and put one foot in front of the other.

And this, I learned: tomorrow will come if you survive today – one step at a time.

But even when there seemed to be no hope left in the world, what should come along but an unexpected gift.

*Was it white bread, Pépé? Surely not a pineapple in that terrible place!*

Oh, no, something much, much better than those.

Because there, I met another prisoner named Kurt, a young German Jew like me. Did Kurt have the keys to open the towering padlocked gates? No. Did he have a shovel to dig under the tangled barbed-wire fence? Not that either. But he gave me the one thing I needed to keep me from giving up. True friendship.

At the beginning of each day, Kurt and I would walk together, talking and sharing our thoughts and hopes. And at the end of each day, Kurt and I would look after each other. If one of us was injured or too sick for work, the other would find food to share – or a scrap of old rag to bind around our frozen feet. I owed it to Kurt to live another day so that I might see him again and look after him. One good friend can be your entire world.

All through the camps, prisoners would secretly show small kindnesses to each other – share a crust of bread, a blanket, a tender embrace.

And this, I know. If you give something, something will come back. Friends, family and kindness, my parents told me, are far more precious than money. A field can be empty, but if you put in the effort to grow something, then you will have a garden.

And who would have thought that the things I learned at school –
the skill to make machines and tools and delicate medical instruments
– would be the 'armour' that helped to protect me. People with my
skills were needed, and so instead of working outside in the freezing
snow and rain, I was sent to work in a factory.

While others laboured in the biting winds, I was shielded by the gift my father had given me when he hid me behind the name of a German orphan. Did my father know he would be protecting me even after he was lost to me? I think he did. So you see? My education did save my life!

The years of war were filled with heartache and fear. Escaping from the camp across borders, scrambling into muddy ditches hiding from soldiers, being caught again . . . So many times I nearly lost my life.

*You were like a cat with nine lives, Pĕpĕ!*

Yes. You would think I was a cat!

In time, the world learned what was happening to the Jews and soldiers came from countries all over the world. They fought bravely and thousands sacrificed their own lives to defeat the Nazis. The Jewish people who had survived were rescued from those dreadful prison camps. Finally, goodness prevailed.

I began to recover, slowly.

One day, lining up for food at a refugee canteen, I saw the most incredible sight – Kurt, my best friend in the world. Here he was, safe and sound!

And then, unbelievably, came a second miracle. The local Jewish newspaper printed a photo of me on a page of those who had survived the Holocaust and hoped to find other family members.

My sister Henni had survived, and we found each other again. The two people dearest to me in the world at that moment had lived through the most terrible of times and now were by my side.

My sister Henni moved to Australia
and in time, I brought my own
family here too.

For a long time, I could not talk about what had happened.
But I met others who had experienced what I had, and together we
shared our stories. Together, we created a place, a museum, so that
people could hear those stories and see the world through our eyes.

What I have to share is not my pain. What I share is my story of a long life made strong with the things that I've learned. Love and kindness, friendship and generosity, curiosity and hope. These things have made me grow from the happiest boy on Earth to the happiest man on Earth.

Now it's time for you to make the world a better place.
One day, then, perhaps it will be you talking to a young friend,
and it will be you who is the happiest person on Earth.

*Eddie's great-grandchildren:*
*Joel, Samuel, Lara, Zoe and Toby.*
*Photo: Giselle Haber*

*Eddie with his belt, the only personal belonging that*
*wasn't taken from him when he entered the camp.*
*Photo: Katherine Griffiths,*
*courtesy Sydney Jewish Museum*

*Eddie and his wife Flore.*

*Eddie with his sons Michael and Andre*
*and their wives Linda and Eva.*

*Eddie on his 90th birthday with*
*his grandchildren Phillip, Carly,*
*Danielle and Marc.*

*Eddie and his good friend Kurt.*

*Eddie and his sister Henni.*

*Eddie with his mother Lina, father Isidore and sister Henni.*